HOMEMADE
Hoodoo

Magic Spells with Easy Ingredients

by
Talia Felix

©2015

HOMEMADE HOODOO

CHAPTERS

CHAPTER ONE
Real Hoodoo

As magical traditions go, hoodoo is a system of fairly recent creation. Officially, the art was made when African slaves and their traditions of magic were brought to the Americas, although the development did not end there as mere African magic displaced. There were more additions, from German magic, from Native American magic, from French magic, from Mexican magic, and eventually even from East Indian and Arabic influences. The resulting jumble of practices became the American standard of folk magic by the end of the 20th century.

Popular as this magic became, many people who worked with this magical art didn't realize that hoodoo was even what they were doing. The word *hoodoo* itself has developed many negative connotations over the last two-hundred years (though not quite as negative as those of its sister, voodoo) and even today some practicing folks would deny hoodoo as their craft if asked, in the belief that hoodoo is an inherently *evil magic.* Additionally, hoodoo's innate adaptability has meant that some people who intended to be practicing another form of magic such as Wicca or New Age would pick up and absorb hoodoo techniques without recognizing them. For example: the 1977 book *The Magic of New Ishtar Power* published by the E.S.P. Lab doesn't use the word hoodoo even once, and focuses mainly on psychic work, spirit work, and chakra energies. Yet at one point it describes "The Ishtar Mating Call Rite" to attract an ideal lover. The technique is to fix a red flannel bag full of basil, myrtle and cinnamon, perfumed with frankincense oil; Women are to carry it on their bosom, men in their pants pocket. Any acknowledged hoodoo practitioner recognizes that this is a *mojo bag* – one of the oldest documented hoodoo charms. This form of charm is perhaps the most well-known secret of hoodoo, as the term *mojo* originates entirely with the practice. Every song about someone having "mojo" or remark about "getting your mojo on" is, technically, referring to the hoodoo mojo bag and its powers – whether or not the speaker realizes this.

With hoodoo practices being so commonplace in the culture of America, they can become "invisible" like the mojo bag, meaning some people are practicing hoodoo without realizing it. There are people who were taught and trained in other magical traditions and who come across hoodoo spells unexpectedly without recognizing it's a system of its own.

This can cause some confusion. For example, in the last few decades Wicca has made some significant headway as a religious practice, to the point that many people – including some actual Wiccan practitioners – believe that all magic is Wicca and is supposed to follow Wiccan rules. They are then appalled when, for example, introduced to a hoodoo style magic spell that calls upon Jesus and the Saints for help in killing someone, or influencing a jury, or some other selfish intention. Wicca wouldn't pray to Christian figures, and Wicca is widely believed to only allow for positive magic. A person who doesn't know better will even claim that such a spell is *fake* because *it doesn't follow Wicca!* This problem extends to people who practice other forms of magic as well: there are simply some practitioners who can't fathom that there are practices other than what version they were particularly taught, and thus accuse anything unfamiliar of being "fake."

Further issues in this vein are to be found when reading the reviews of popular and important books of hoodoo spells. Some of these are very traditional pieces, like the *Black and White Magic of Marie Laveau*, a.k.a. *The Life and Works of Marie Laveau* that's been in circulation since at least the 1920s and has influenced hundred or even thousands of practitioners – but certain people unfamiliar with the practice wind up accusing the books of being "fake" or of existing "just to sell products." This problem stems from the way post-

1920 hoodoo puts a significant emphasis on premade ingredients, which practitioners of other magical traditions may find odd or even suspicious. People accustomed to other popular magical practices may be in the habit of making their own ingredients or of using easy to find natural products, and can complain a blue streak when presented with a hoodoo spell that requires using products like *John the Conqueror Oil* and *Come to Me Incense.* An exact quote from a review left for one of my favorite hoodoo spellbooks on Amazon moans, "This book seems like an advertisement for products in a store." I've even been accused myself, by reviewers of my books, of having only written them to sell products in my shop (Note: I don't have a shop.)

Before 1920, hoodoo had a greater emphasis on hand-gathered herbal ingredients but still included products which needed to be bought, like whiskey and certain perfumes. Things turned after World War One when a combination of factors led to an increase in purchasing the products needed for conjure workings from spiritual supply houses. These reasons included more practitioners moving to urban areas where wild-growing herbs were harder to find, better supply routes encouraging sellers to promote their goods farther afield, new technologies making the supplies cheaper to produce, and a general change in the American culture at large which found people buying more products ready-made.

Picture it: once upon a time, people made their own ketchup, their own butter, baked their own bread, produced macaroni from hand-mixed white sauce with carefully home-grated cheese stirred in over hand-cut noodles. While there are still some people who do these things today, nobody looks at it as a scam if a cookbook provides a recipe requiring a spoonful of bought Tabasco sauce and a package of cheddar cheese instead of instructing on how to produce these at home from scratch. Does anyone really think that mom's chocolate chip cookie recipe, with its requirement for a package of chocolate chips, was simply something she "made up" to sell chocolate? Of course not. Likewise, it's *not* a sign of scamming or fakeness or ulterior motives if a hoodoo spell requires the use of premade formulas and products. If you think that readymade conjure formulas are only about "ripping people off", take this into account: there was recently a video circulating online from *How To Make Everything*, which saw a man make a normal chicken sandwich entirely from scratch. He grew his own wheat, gathered his own salt, killed his own chicken, etc., etc. By doing it this way, it ultimately cost him $1,500 to make one sandwich! We can conclude here that doing everything yourself is not necessarily a cash-saver.

In spite of the utility of readymade formulas, sometimes a situation will come where there isn't availability of necessary conjure products. Maybe a spell needs to be done right away but no suppliers are nearby, or maybe the only available supplies are untrustworthy for some reason or another. (Shoddy ingredients are, sadly, common to find from some spiritual suppliers.) Or, maybe you want to try out some hoodoo magic but are not yet comfortable with buying all those fancy products before you have the hang of it. Or something else may compel you altogether – but whatever the reason, you've come to this book, and this book's aim is to provide proper hoodoo spells utilizing no premade "magic formulas." Everything given in this book should be available outside of an occult shop, in any reasonably sized town that offers something more than a Walmart to shop at. (And even if you do have nothing but Walmart, the spells in this book will still go pretty far.) While some of the ingredients might be of a modern sort, this style of hoodoo where the practitioners uses common ingredients that are easy to find is very traditional and hearkens back to the most old fashioned techniques.

Here's the thing: unless you grow all your own herbs from found seeds and possess your own distilling supplies and sculpt your own containers out of clay which you gathered yourself and you weave your own cloth bags and mine your own minerals, you are likely going to have to buy something from *someone* to perform spells, even these ones. Hoodoo tradition is not mere chants or visualization. In most cases, you have to use physical items in order to direct the magic.

The essential concept behind hoodoo is that there are spirits or forces around us which can be moved to act for our benefit. They may be worship-worthy entities like gods, or simple natural powers and phenomena, but to work them according to your own will you must utilize and direct them in certain ways. This is normally done by the application of herbs, minerals, waters, pigments and other *material objects.* Some people conceptualize the need for these objects as offerings to the entities, others think the objects *are* the entities or else a powerful link to them. It doesn't really matter. Whatever way you want to conceptualize it, the physical items are essential in hoodoo practice. A glop of peanut butter is not a PB&J. Magical prayers or chants might be used within the tradition but by themselves are not necessarily hoodoo, and those "magic words" which have worked their way into standard hoodoo practices (such as reciting psalms to achieve certain ends) can be easily traced as borrowings from earlier and outside practices (such as kabbalist magic.)

Since many hoodoo magic spells operate by way of physical objects which are perceived as living – what is one to do with the resulting magical spell devices that are meant to "work"? Traditionally, the answer is to place the charms in specific locations that relate to the intention.

If a charm is meant to affect yourself, you might carry it with you all or most of the time. If it's to affect someone else, you might try to place it on them. Hiding things in their clothing or belongings is a common technique for this.

When one deposits a spell at a house, it should be the home of the person the spell is meant to influence. So, if it's a spell to help yourself, you keep the charm at your own house (or business or workplace). If your spell is to influence somebody else through magic, you will hide the item at their house (or business or workplace) or as near to it as you can get. It is perfectly fine to conceal the charm; it need not be plainly visible.

Magic items for any purpose can be buried in the middle of the crossroads (or dropped at the crossroads, if the road is paved. If it's a large item, many folks like to leave it on the corner facing the middle of the crossroads, so as not to disrupt traffic.) Any intersection, whether paved or dirt, whether for foot traffic or motor vehicles, is a crossroads. Crossroads are a magical "in between" place where various realities can come together to create new 'paths' for your life, thus they have their special power.

If your spells are for beneficial purposes, they can be deposited into a river or other body of water. Water purifies and blesses, and for love spells, success spells or money spells it can cause things to 'flow' your way. In spells for the influence other people's thoughts, it can make their thoughts 'flow' or 'drift' your way.

If you spell is meant to do great harm to someone, it might go into a graveyard. Sometimes the objects are just tossed or dropped into the cemetery by the practitioner, whereas some folks take the time to bury the items in the graveyard someplace. It might be appropriate to bring a gift or symbolic payment of a few coins for the dead, particularly if you place the object on a grave.

All these places for depositing and disposing of spells have a particular significance. Because of this, it is never felt to be acceptable to throw your magical items in the trash. Throwing in the trash just sends the spiritual message that you're disgusted with the spell and don't want it anymore, and so this should only ever be done with items where that is genuinely the case. This is especially true of any empowered items, such as mojo bags or blessed herbs – when you wish to dispose of them, these *must* be ritually buried (by land or water) or respectfully burned, because there is understood to be an indwelling spirit in the item which must be given a proper release.

With this basic understanding of what makes hoodoo into hoodoo, we can begin to work with a version simplified to be accessible even to those who don't have a lot of access to fancy magical supplies. There's no need to memorize botany and go tearing up the neighbor's lavender bush to get the things you need. The kitchen witch and do-it-yourselfer can be content with practicing a genuine form of this folk magic that doesn't require significantly more work than a home-cooked meal. Hoodoo is possible to make at home, and this book will show you how.

CHAPTER TWO
Formulas

Formulas of hoodoo are important to the modern practice. Nowadays, these mixtures are commonly bought readymade from a supplier; but those who know how it's done will easily be able to make their own. In this chapter are recipes for some of the more vital of the conjure products, which ought to be had by any practitioner.

When it comes to magical formulas, a few things should be explained. Firstly, *there is no one recipe for these products*, just like there's no one single recipe for chocolate cake. You can make the same thing a lot of different ways, and if you see recipes that differ from the one you know, it's just another way of achieving the same intent. The main matter to beware is recipes which stray too greatly from required standards – if we are to repeat the chocolate cake metaphor, you'd know a recipe for chocolate cake had something wrong with it if there were no mention of chocolate anywhere in the ingredient list. Some products like John the Conqueror, Van Van, Master and Has No Hanna have names which refer to key ingredients, which must be included or at least thoughtfully replaced with an equivalent in any legitimate recipe for the product.

The next thing to keep in mind is that there are no quantities needed for most magical formulas. Once, I had a spellcast client from my online business to whom I sent a recipe for an oil. She wrote me back complaining that I'd forgotten to include the amounts. However, no, that was no mistake – there are no amounts in this type of magic! When making a recipe, an easy way to start is with equal parts of each ingredient, and then to add more of whatever needs more until you've got it as you want it. Even occult suppliers often do not use a set recipe for their products, which can lead to some disappointment when trying to buy the same item again and again from a manufacturer – you get a totally different version each time. When blending ingredients, it is important to be aware of any irritating or hazardous substances and to make certain to minimize them appropriately. Don't make a bath for yourself that's going to use fifteen drops of pure cinnamon oil per bath, for example; but one or two drops of cinnamon oil diluted in a full bathtub might be acceptable if you don't have terribly sensitive skin. Using cinnamon leaf oil in lieu of regular cinnamon oil is even better, if you're trying to prepare a skin-safe blend.

For the purpose of this book, I'm offering condition formulas based on essential oils, as these oils are easier to come by than many of the straight herbs which are used in conjure – obscure things like deerstongue, devil's shoestring and master root that one rarely sees for sale outside an occult shop. Essential oils can normally be had at health food stores and sometimes at herbal medicine shops, head shops or gift shops.

It is important to understand the difference between an essential oil and a fragrance oil – *essential oils* are the extracted oils taken directly from plants. *Fragrance oils* are artificial composites made from scented chemicals to approximate the smells of plant oils. Both have a history of use in magic, but there are some people who believe only the essential oils should be employed for spellwork. However, you should be warned that many sellers of essential oils are really selling fragrance oils, possibly without even realizing it. This is especially common when you buy the oils from flea markets, mall kiosks, eBay, or other such small sellers, who seem often to have either misunderstood what they were buying, or who bought their stock from a disreputable supplier. You can sometimes smoke out the frauds by their prices – if a person is selling rose oil or jasmine oil for less than $30 an ounce, there's no possible way it's pure essential oil; it's either diluted, adulterated or artificial. Another way I've caught fakes is when they sell items with names like "Egyptian Sandalwood" that don't exist botanically

17

(Sandalwood only grows in India, Nepal, Pakistan or Australia.) There are also some plants like banana, honeysuckle and lilac that do not produce essential oils at all, and seeing them available should send up a red flag that you're perusing fragrances not essentials. The final trick requires a bit of knowledge of what the essential oils really smell like, but if you sniff it and recognize that the odor is markedly different from the natural essence (usually meaning 'too good' as essential oils often have something of a medicinal tinge, whilst artificial fragrances are made to be attractive perfume scents) you can judge it's not true plant oil or that it has been adulterated.

OILS

Hoodoo condition oils are normally not made from the straight essential oils, but rather from the oils or herbs mixed into a carrier oil like almond, olive, jojoba, mineral oil, or whatever you like. Even plain old cooking oil works. I recommend using 15 to 20 drops of essential oil for every half ounce of carrier. This is used to dress candles or the body, and to feed mojo bags and other talismans.

BATHS AND WASHES

The simplest way to make a bath wash is to add your essential oil blend directly to the tub, but many people prefer to mix the oils with epsom salts as a carrier. Use 20 to 30 drops of oil to 1/3 cup epsom salt, to make enough for one bath in a full tub of water (or use half the amount of oil if your tub is small or if you're using a mixture that's heavy on irritating oils.) Old time recipes for bath and floor washes would mix the oils in a base of 90% rubbing alcohol: add 15 to 20 drops to half an ounce of alcohol, and add the mix to the tub. Bath washes can also be used as floor and laundry washes by adding the mixtures respectively to the mop-bucket or the rinse water.

SACHET POWDERS

To make a sachet powder, mix 2 tablespoons baking soda with 4 tablespoons corn starch. Add 5 to 10 drops of essential oil and mix very thoroughly, till all lumps are smooth and the oil is evenly absorbed and distributed. This powder can be applied to the body, carried in mojo bags, dusted about the house or in the path of people you'd like to influence, or used to dress candles. It can even be added to the tub in lieu of bath blends.

ALCOHOL PERFUMES

Alcohol perfumes have recently declined in popularity but are actually as traditional in hoodoo as the perfume oils. Many older formulas originated as alcohol perfumes – Van

Van and Essence of Bend Over are among these. The perfumes are easy to wear on the body, spray on clothes or pour into a bath or floor wash. They can also be spritzed as a room spray. Use 1 part of your essential oil blend to 5 parts alcohol, and combine thoroughly. A perfumers grade alcohol is best, but 91% isopropyl alcohol will work if you don't mind the smell being altered slightly.

Here follow some standard recipes that no practitioner should be without:

VAN VAN - A lucky oil with reputed properties of undoing blockages, reversing bad luck and enhancing all positive magic. All-purpose for any positive working.

lemongrass
cinnamon
rosemary

RETURN TO ME – used to draw back a lost lover or friend.

rose
tuberose or patchouli
lavender or balsam fir

FAST LUCK – for good luck in a hurry, especially money luck and love luck. Can be used in lieu of love-drawing potions.

bergamot

lemongrass

cinnamon

PROTECTION – for protection against jinxes and against general misfortunes and negative people.

patchouli

sandalwood or cedarwood

lilac or rose

UNCROSSING – for obliterating jinxes, removing negativity and undoing spells that have been cast on you. Also used preemptively to protect against jinxes.

lime or lemon

rosemary

HAS NO HANNA – an all-purpose luck formula, for bringing in *the good life*.

jasmine

COMMAND AND COMPEL – to gain influence over others. Can be used on one's self to generally increase the ability to sway others, or can be targeted at a specific person to try to force their cooperation.

calamus

bergamot

vetiver

COME TO ME – a love-drawing formula, able to be used generally to attract new people or can be used to draw a specific person.

rose

jasmine

orange

BLACK MAGIC OIL – for all negative works, and can be used to enhance neutral workings like love-drawing and protection.

patchouli

frankincense

myrrh

jasmine

cypress

black pepper

PEACE – to calm disturbed conditions and settle emotions. Also useful for uncrossing.

sandalwood

clary sage

lavender

MONEY DRAWING – to attract money through all methods, including gambling and speculation.

cinnamon

nutmeg

peppermint or wintergreen

There is a belief amongst some practitioners that "consecrating" or "empowering" the mixture is necessary before putting it to use in rituals. It is not a universal belief, and it's particularly unnecessary if you perceive the ingredients themselves to be the source of the powers. Nevertheless, it is popular enough that it's become fairly standard in modern practice, probably influenced by the rise of Ceremonial Magic in the 19th and 20th centuries where the ritual of the blessing is what's important to provide power, rather than the physical substance. Pre-20th century hoodoo spells do not explicitly reference this in relation to formulas, and any special instructions instead tend to put their emphasis upon how the individual herbs that were used in the mixture were gathered and prepped – though it can be fairly said that pre-made formulas were altogether less common before the 20th century and so there are limited survivals on record.

In any case, if you wish to empower your formulations in the modern style, methods for doing so include:

- placing the container in sunlight or moonlight for several hours
- smoking the container in incense, or burning incense nearby while you make the mixture
- holding the container in your hands and visualizing that it is filled with energy
- reciting magic words or prayers over the containers, such as psalms or the Our Father
- setting the items near a burning candle

I'll go ahead and say that I don't do any of this, and I really don't find my formulas to be hurt by the omission: I take the view that it's the ingredients that matter, not the faith. I was once a bit simultaneously amused and annoyed to read a book review for a formulary I published, where somebody accused me of having withheld the magical empowerment instructions in order to "protect my secrets"! Sounds fancy, but no – the only reason it was left out is because it wasn't ever there to begin with. I personally find my mixtures come out best if I don't think too much about them, and I am not alone in this: I once took part in a happy discussion with some other practitioners where we agreed that distractedly making our mixtures while watching TV seemed to produce the best effects. (It was never said explicitly by anyone, but the concept seems to be that rather than empowering a mixture, too much thought can actually hinder the mixture's ability to function – an oft mentioned phenomenon called "worrying a spell to death.") Hoodoo isn't really the kind of magic to get into if you're obsessed with romantic ideas of The Great Magickal Art. It is classified as "low magic" and will often tend toward what is simple over what is fancy.

CHAPTER THREE
Herbs

Herbal ingredients are of great importance to the hoodoo practitioner – sometimes they are even considered to the be most powerful active force of the entire spell. Getting your hands on the right herbs is essential for your practice. Your average grocery store may not carry devil's shoestring or master of the woods, but your spice rack is surely loaded with many effective materials for magical intent. Additionally, some stores will carry medicinal teas and herbal supplement pills, which can be used in place of the bulk plant material. Simply crush the pills or tear open the tea bags and use the contents just like any other magical plant.

There are a few different ways to use herbs for enhancing your magical work, but common methods include powdering them and rolling oiled candles in the dust before burning them, or mixing the pulverized herbs with condition powders to add extra benefits, boiling them to make baths or washes, scattering them about the home, or adding the herbs to mojo bags.

COMMON CULINARY HERBS

Allspice – for money drawing and for good luck.

Basil – for purification, for luck-bringing, and for money drawing.

Bay Leaves – used to bring victory and success.

Caraway – protection against jinxes and against illness.

Celery Seed – for psychic vision.

Cayenne Pepper or Chile Flakes – used for protection, for uncrossing, for enemy work, and sometimes to "turn up the heat" on a spell that needs to work quickly.

Cinnamon – for money, for love, and also for protection.

Clove – love and friendship.

Coriander seed – used for love, fidelity, and also for court cases.

Cumin – for protection and for peace.

Dill Weed or Dill Seed – used for court cases and legal work.

Fennel – for protection and for keeping away unwanted attention from the law.

Ginger – used for lust spells, and also used for protection. Like cayenne pepper it can add "heat" to any working.

Marjoram – to keep away unwanted people and protect from jinxes.

Mustard Seed – black or brown mustard is used for enemy work and to cause confusion. White or yellow mustard is used for protection and uncrossing.

Nutmeg – for drawing money and for inducing lust.

Oregano – keep away unwanted people.

Parsley – good luck and money drawing.

Rosemary – for purification, spiritual cleansing, healing and protection. Reputed to strengthen memory and for this reason sometimes considered good towards love and loyalty.

Thyme – money drawing and repels misfortune.

COMMON HERBAL TEAS

Chamomile – use for money drawing

Dandelion – use for peace and protection

Licorice – for command and influence

Mint – for cleansing, mental ability, and money drawing

Echinacea – use for protection, uncrossing

Ginger – lust-inspiring and also protective

Ginseng – love drawing for men

St. John's Wort – for happiness and good fortune

Lemon – use for purifying and uncrossing

Lavender – for love, health and peace

Fennel – for protection from trouble

Hibiscus– for love

Lemon Balm – removes unwanted influences

Linden – cleansing and healing

Nettle – for uncrossing

Coffee – used to repel witchcraft

It has been warned that the magical significance of herbs is variable. What the herb is used for in one style of magic might not apply to another. Because hoodoo is something of a mishmash of other magical practices, plant symbolism is especially variable. I've listed here traditional associations but, if you use a plant differently or if it represents something different to you, by all means stick with what you know – I was once told by a wise practitioner, "no matter how traditional it is, if it doesn't mean the same thing to you, it'll never work." *Of course, don't think you can now use this advice to assign new meanings to herbs willy-nilly*; simply bear in mind that if, say, frankincense has always been a purifying herb to you and you simply can't imagine how or why it would be able to work as a hexing ingredient, then don't worry about it and just use something else that you think would work as a hexing ingredient instead of trying to go forward with an ingredient that makes no sense to you. Also take this advice as a way to be more open-minded about the meanings and uses of herbs, for situations where you might be able to overcome a prejudice – especially if it's in the name of sticking to a tradition.

CHAPTER FOUR
Candle Magic

As hoodoo traditions go, candles are a fairly new contribution to the art. You can often identify spells as being post-1915 by the use of candles, though there are occasional rituals of an earlier date that employ them. Modern hoodoo uses colored candles for various rituals. The generally approved color system is this:

Black - often used for harmful purposes, it is also used for protection, removal of blockages, dispelling negativity, and sometimes for strong domination.

White - used for purification, peace, protection, spirituality and holiness. Can also be used for marriage.

Red - very versatile and very traditional, it can be used for power, love, lust, command, money, protection and reversal of jinxes, as well as for doing harm. Use this color if in doubt.

Blue - for blessings, healing, protection, and for love.

Green - almost always used for money; also by extension for gambling luck, business success and job-getting.

Yellow - for luck, success, attraction, money.

Purple - for power, mastery, wisdom, success, command, domination, and for jobs and business.

Orange - for command, power, positive energy, opening the way and removing blockages.

Brown - often used for court case and legal work. Also for special favors and influence.

Pink - the only pastel color used commonly, it is employed for love work, and sometimes for gaining favoritism, or for healing.

While the tinting of wax with color goes back thousands of years, colored candles had to be specially made until recent times. Even now, white candles are the standard in most places. Because of this, a white or uncolored candle can be used to replace any color of hoodoo candle if you are unable to find one in a suitable hue. It is also possible to improvise candle colors by using markers or shoe polish to color in a white candle, although this practice doesn't work so well if you intend to dress the candle with oil, as the candle dressing will rub away your pigment.

Gift shops often carry a selection of colored candles, however, they more often than not will already be scented with fragrances that are popular as air fresheners. Although they are not made with occult practice in mind, sometimes these scents can be put to work for you in magic. Here's a list of some popular candle perfumes and how you can use them:

Ocean Breeze/Ocean Mist – for purification
Black Cherry – for love
Vanilla/French Vanilla – for luck
Apple/Apple Cinnamon – for love
Cotton/Linen – for cleansing, for peace, or for love work
Cinnamon/Cinnamon Bun – for money and business
Lilac – for love and for protection
Pine/Fir – for money, for protection, and for cleansing
Lavender – for peace, healing and for love
Sandalwood – for peace, cleansing, jinx removal and for blessing
Eucalyptus – for purification
Coconut – for influence

Many of these fragrances are also available in room sprays and air fresheners, and can be used for the same purposes. These type of scents are usually *not* made from essential oils, so if you feel it is important that the ingredients be of natural origin, you might not wish to use them.

Depending on where you live, you might be able to find certain types of glass encased candles with affixed labels at your local drugstore or grocery. This is more typical in areas inhabited by a large population of Mexicans or Catholics. Usually the candles will be decorated with pictures of Catholic saints or Christian religious imagery, though a few other popular spiritual candles might sneak into the selection, like a "Lucky Lotto" candle or a "Reversible." You should check on what is available to you. The imagery on the candle is often suggestive of the use – for example, Sacred Heart of Mary or Sacred Heart of Jesus has a prominent image of a heart, and so these are sometimes repurposed for spells relating to heart troubles, be they literal (health problems) or figurative (romantic matters.) Guardian Angel candles are used for protection. St. Martin Caballero candles are used to draw business (because St. Martin is portrayed stopping for a beggar to show him generosity.) You do not necessarily need to petition the religious figures on the candles in order to use the candle, though spiritualists usually consider it to be good manners to do so.

If you don't want to use the religious candles, you can sometimes find glass encased candles without labels for sale. These can be taken home, and you can draw or print your own pictures to tape onto the glass yourself, thereby creating whatever kind of candle you want. You can also buy any religious candle with a paper label and scrub the label off at home with a scouring pad and water, then use the candle plain or with your own custom label. These candles are often dressed with oils by either rubbing a few drops across the exposed top part of the candle wax, or else by boring holes into the wax with a skewer, nail or pencil and pouring the oil down into the holes (3, 4 or 7 holes are traditional depending on whose technique is used.)

Occultists love to use figural candles or image candles, these being candles that are pre-formed into a shape. Human figures (male and female) and skulls are some of the most popular. Candles like these are used to represent the subject of the spell being cast. It's unusual to find such candles outside of an occult store, but you can make your own by simply buying any large wax candle and carving it into shape by yourself with a knife or with heated sculpting tools – pillar style candles will tend to work best for this purpose. You don't need to be a Donatello when doing this. Even the quality of the sculpture on the commercial candles isn't all that great. As long as it looks recognizably like the shape that you're after, your candles will work fine.

Some basics on candle magic: never use a "used" (i.e. previously lit) candle for a spell, and never reuse a spell candle unless it is to be for a spell of *exactly* the same purpose. Typically you want to allow your candles to burn all the way out during your spell, so having leftovers shouldn't be a common problem. If your candle goes out unexpectedly or prematurely, you can relight it up to three times – if it continues to go out, consider that the universe is outright telling you "No" to your petition. And of course – always burn your candles in a safe place, away from paper, plastic or fabric that could catch alight, and where the candle can sit securely without risk of being bumped or knocked over. Choose a space free from pets, children or visitors. Having a tray or a plate beneath your candle, to catch any dripping wax, is advised.

CHAPTER FIVE
Incense and Air Freshener

The use of incense in hoodoo rituals is another practice that belongs mostly to the 20th and 21st centuries, evidently having been inspired by the practices of Ceremonial magic which filtered down into hoodoo through the large occult suppliers, which sold public domain books about magical practice alongside candles and other common mystic supplies. Whether or not incense is legitimate "old time" hoodoo, it definitely is part of the practice now.

Many drug stores and groceries will carry a small selection of incense, typically in stick form. Cone incense is another typical form, and occasionally one might find powdered incense, of which there are two potential types: noncombustible and self-lighting. The noncombustible needs to be burned on a piece of charcoal or other heat source in order to create smoke, whereas the self-lighting will burn if it's merely squeezed into a conical shape and lit with a match.

There are many different recipes for incense, but most of the stick and cone incense you'll find on the general market is made by buying 'blank' incense sticks or cones from a manufacturer and then soaking them in fragrance oils. Unless you're shopping at a Whole Foods or other such natural grocer, it's unlikely they will contain any genuine essential oils or plant products beyond the wood flour used in forming the blanks.

The type of shop that you visit will have a great effect on what kind of incense fragrances are available to you. The selection at my own local drugstore consisted of incense scented to knockoff designer perfumes (*Giorgio, Drakkar Noir, Eternity* and *Obsession*) and a few single note scents (vanilla, rose, sandalwood, coconut, cinnamon, strawberry.) In comparison, a trip to the nearest natural grocer found many exotic incenses from India and Japan as well as some locally made material, with scents ranging all the way from *Sage & Cedar* to *Morning Zen*.

As far as incenses which will be suitable to use in hoodoo magical practice, single note fragrances (or at least, those which name their primary ingredients) are preferable. They are more versatile and are easier to choose appropriately. *Moss Garden* incense could be made out of anything and useful for who knows what, but *Cinnamon* incense is useful for everything that the herb cinnamon is fit for.

Your local selection of scents, naturally, will vary; but here are some common fragrances you might find:

Allspice – for money drawing and for good luck

Apple/Apple Cinnamon – for love

Basil – for purification, for luck-bringing, and for money drawing

Black Cherry – for love

Chamomile – use for money drawing

Cinnamon – for money and for love, and also for protection.

Clove – love and friendship

Coconut – for influence

Coffee – used to repel witchcraft

Cotton/Linen – for cleansing, for peace, or for love work

Eucalyptus – for purification

Ginger – used for lust spells, and also used for protection. It can also add "heat" to any working

Lavender – for peace, healing and for love

Lemon – use for purifying and uncrossing

Lemongrass – a multipurpose scent and the basis of the famous "Van Van" perfume. It is luck bringing and jinx breaking, as well as being said to increase the power of other ingredients

Lilac – for love and for protection

Mint – for cleansing, mental ability, and money drawing

Nag Champa – an all-purpose fragrance

Nutmeg – for drawing money and for inducing lust.

Ocean Breeze/Ocean Mist – for purification

Pine/Fir – for money, for protection, and for cleansing

Rosemary – for purification, spiritual cleansing, healing and protection. Reputed to strengthen memory and for this reason sometimes considered good towards love and loyalty

Sandalwood – for peace, cleansing, jinx removal and for blessing

Strawberry – for attraction

Vanilla/French Vanilla – for luck

TO USE HOODOO INCENSE

In the hoodoo tradition, incense can either be burnt as an emphatic alongside another working (such as a candle spell) or it can be used by itself. When burning incense on its own, many people will put a written petition paper under the censer before lighting the incense; it's then believed that the smoke from the burning incense either carries the message out to the spirits or to the world, or else that the smoke and scent will alert helpful spirits and draw their attention to your petition. Some people might burn incense and blow the smoke in the direction where the person they wish to effect is dwelling, thus sending the smoke and its influence to them. There is also the belief that the scent of the perfumes will influence your surroundings, and in that case, one might regularly burn an incense in order to improve or maintain a condition at home. An example of this would be burning a good luck incense every day to ensure continuous good luck.

TO USE HOODOO AIR FRESHENER

Some people can't abide the smoke from incense, or else live in a situation where others would complain if smokey incense were being burned. Spray air fresheners are useful to these people. They can be employed to perfume the house so as to give favorable scent vibrations to the property, or they can be used by spraying in the direction of the person one wishes to influence. Petition papers cannot be used the way they are with burned incense, but some people are known to speak their petition aloud while spraying air freshener through the room in a shape of two intersecting lines, in order to produce magical effect.

CHAPTER SIX
Love Spells

Love spells are some of the most popular and oft requested spells there are. While some people view them as immoral for being "coercive" or "against free will" others feel that using a spell to aid in love is no different than using fancy perfumes or good grooming or fine manners to win someone's heart. Just like when buying an expensive gift in hopes of impressing your desired mate, spells cannot be depended upon to always produce the desired result. Love forever remains a gamble whether there's magic involved or not.

It is generally said that the best day to perform love spells is on Friday, but if the spell lasts for multiple days or if you cannot wait for Friday, it will not be detrimental to do it on some other day.

1. Make Them Sweet On You

- 9 candles (white, pink or red)
- sugar, saccharin or any other sweetener
- photograph of the target
- writing pen (red ink is best)

1. Have a printed photograph of your desired lover. Write their name and birthdate on the photograph, and draw hearts in the four corners of the picture. Place the photo on a plate, tray or any other suitable altar space you want to create.

2. When the picture is ready, take the sugar and, using a clockwise motion, sprinkle it over the photograph in a circle. It is alright if the sugar obscures the picture.

3. Put your first candle on top of the photo. State aloud your command and state the target's name in so doing, e.g. "Jon Jonson, you will be sweet to me and think sweetly of me." Light the candle as you say your wish.

4. Let the candle burn itself all the way out.

5. The next day, repeat these steps with a new candle. Continue to repeat till all candles are used – a total of nine days.

2. Make Their Heart Follow You

- a square of paper, approx. 4"x4"
- ink pen (red is best)
- powdered cinnamon
- a scrap of cloth, any color

1. Write the target's name on the paper three times in ink.
2. Place a small pinch of the powdered cinnamon on the paper.
3. Drawing the paper toward you (to symbolize the target's affections moving toward you) fold it in half, so that the cinnamon is inside. Fold the paper this way a second time so that the cinnamon is enveloped by the paper.
4. Wrap the paper in a small piece of cloth – this is a practical step to help protect the paper and keep everything together. Do not wrap the cloth too thickly around the paper, you want to keep everything nice and thin.
5. Place the resulting packet in your right shoe. Wear the shoe every day to make the person's heart follow where you go.

3. Love Drawing Bath

- orange (dried peel or fresh fruit)
- lemon (dried peel or fresh fruit)
- lavender (tea or dried herb)
- hibiscus (tea or dried herb)
- rose (fresh flowers or dried herb)
- carnation (fresh flowers)
- cinnamon stick
- vanilla bean
- sugar

1. This is best done on a full moon.
2. Chop any fresh ingredients, then mix everything together in a large pot or dish.
3. Cover the ingredients with boiling water and allow everything to steep together for nine minutes.
4. Strain the mixture. The resulting liquid can be added to your bath water to attract lovers.

4. The Apple of Love

- three hairs from your target
- three hairs from yourself
- an apple - the more pristine its appearance, the better
- two strips of paper, about 2" by 3"
- a calligraphy pen or small paintbrush
- two sharp wooden toothpicks
- rose oil
- rose petals
- bay leaves
- some cloth (red, blue or pink is best)
- string or thread

1. Begin by drawing a small amount of your own blood by whatever means are appropriate.
2. Using the pen or brush, take some of the blood as ink and write on one piece of paper the word *Scheva*.
3. On the second paper, write your first and last name, then on the next line write the first and last name of your target.
4. Put the hairs together. If they are long enough, use them to wrap the two papers facing each other;

45

otherwise you can fold the hairs sandwiched inside the papers.

5. Cut the apple in two and scoop out the core. Put the papers inside the hollow, and rejoin the apple halves.

6. Anoint your toothpicks with some rose oil. Use these fixed toothpicks to secure the two apple halves back together.

7. Preheat your oven to 150 degrees F. Place your apple on a baking sheet and roast it in the oven until it is dried, which will probably take several hours.

8. Take your dried apple and wrap it in the cloth along with your rose petals and bay leaves. Secure the cloth with thread or string.

9. Hide the finished charm under the mattress of your beloved.

5. Attract New Love

- basil (fresh or dried)
- rose petals (fresh or dried)
- lavender (tea or dried herb)
- licorice (tea or dried herb)
- a square of red cloth, about 6" each side
- a string

1. Finely chop any fresh ingredients. Combine 1 teaspoon of each herb together.
2. Place the herb mixture in the center of your cloth.
3. Draw the corners of the cloth together, forming a little sack. Wrap a length of string tightly about 1 to 2 inches up from the base to secure the herbs, and tie the string with three knots.
4. Wear the resulting pouch from another string around your neck, and it is said that its scent will draw you a new lover.

6. Call Love To Your Home

- cinnamon scented candles - one for each room of your house
- cinnamon oil or flavoring
- sugar
- liquid bluing (available in laundry aisle)

1. Ideally you should prepare your home with a good cleaning, sweeping the floors and straightening up any clutter.
2. When ready, prepare a wash mixture of the bluing, cinnamon essence and sugar in a large bucket of water. Use this water to wash all the floors, walls and furniture in your home. Be particularly sure to wash the doorframes, since these are the entrances of your house.
3. Pour out any remaining wash water in front of your house.
4. Place a cinnamon fragrance candle in each room in a safe burning spot. Light each candle while declaring aloud your wish for love to come into your home. Let the candles burn out.

7. Provoke Passionate Love

- powdered nutmeg

To do this spell, you will need access to the shoes of your target – shoes that they will continue to wear are best, but a discarded pair is acceptable. At the stroke of midnight, sprinkle a little of the nutmeg into his or her shoes while declaring aloud your command "Love me!" This spell works by foottrack magic to make them crazy with love for you.

8. Restore Fading Love

- ground cloves
- ground cinnamon
- ground cardamom
- rosewater OR rose petal tea
- a shirt belonging to the target

1. At midnight, combine the spices together with the rosewater in a bowl. Allow them to soak together till 3 AM.
2. Take the shirt and wash it in this herbal mixture. Dry the shirt and have the target continue to wear it to inspire them with fresh love.

Note. A version of this spell was reported in Henri Gamache's *Magic of Herbs* with the addition of Quranic verses. Instead of letting the herbs soak from midnight, the operator was to recite the Surah Ya-Sin backwards seven times over the mixture. The Ya-Sin is said to be the "heart of the Quran."

9. Return A Lost Lover

- lavender essential oil
- paper, measuring about 3" x 5"
- permanent marker
- a tall drinking glass
- 7 candles (white or pink are best)

1. Write the absent lover's full name seven times on the paper.
2. Put the paper into a drinking glass and fill the glass with water.
3. Pour two tablespoons of lavender oil into the cup (it's fine if it floats on top.)
4. Put the glass underneath your bed and don't disturb it till your target returns.
5. With the marker, write your lover's name on each candle three times.
6. Each day, burn one candle in front of a window, until you've burned all the candles.

10. A Love Lamp

- a pumpkin or squash, as round as possible
- cinnamon oil
- rose oil
- olive oil
- honey
- five copper pennies
- gold glitter
- floating wick
- photo of the target

1. Take the pumpkin and cut off its top third. Discard the top. Clean the pumpkin out with a spoon or scraper to make a sort of bowl.
2. Fill the pumpkin with the glitter, pennies, honey and oils. Be especially generous with the olive oil, as this is the primary fuel for the lamp.
3. Place the pumpkin atop the photograph of the person.
4. Add the wick and light it. Allow it to burn for as long as it will do – it's said that the desired lover will contact you before the lamp burns out.

CHAPTER SEVEN
Hate Spells

Hoodoo has a popular reputation for being all about "evil black magic." While there is clearly more to it than that, the fact remains that it is a tradition which does allow for such spells to be cast. Being a folk magic system as opposed to a religion or lifestyle, it allows the user to decide what kind of intentions they are comfortable with casting spells for. There are still some practitioners who will not perform work of this nature if their own personal beliefs forbid it. Others are willing to do such work freely, figuring that it's "up to God" whether it succeeds or not, or feeling that their reasons for wanting the work are morally justified.

It is said that the best days for performing spells of harmful intent are Saturdays and Tuesdays.

The spells given in Chapter 11 will protect a person from the effects of these kinds of workings.

HOMEMADE HOODOO

1. Break Up A Couple

- a lemon
- a knife
- cayenne pepper
- black pepper
- photos of the couple - a separate picture of each
- pen (red or black ink is best)
- needle and thread

1. Begin by writing the name and, if known, the birthdate of each person of their respective photograph.
2. Take the knife and cut a deep slit into the lemon. Do not sever the lemon in two.
3. Sprinkle the peppers inside the slit in the lemon.
4. Place the two photos back-to-back to one another. Fold them up, always pushing the paper away from yourself, till they are small enough to fit inside the slit in the lemon.
5. Place the pictures in the slit and sprinkle some more pepper on top of them.
6. Using the needle and thread, sew the lemon shut again with X shaped stitches.

7. This lemon is best if buried at the couple's house, but if that isn't possible, it can be buried in a graveyard.

NOTE: A version of this spell done with salt and pepper instead of the cayenne and black pepper is commended especially for cases where the couple is only being held together by witchcraft already. Also, a variant using salt alone can be done as part of a "Cut and Clear" type working wherein a person willingly wishes to end their romantic relationship but needs the assistance of magic to weaken their own lingering attachments.

2. To Kill Someone

- photograph of victim
- 9 nails
- a hammer

1. Find a tree and locate its north side. This spell is best done at dawn or midnight.
2. With the first of your nails, nail the photo to the tree on its north side.
3. Every day at the same time, come back to the tree and drive another nail into the photo. until you have used all of the nails. It is said that the victim will grow sick and die.

3. A Jinxing Bottle

- a bottle or jar with lid (such as a cleaned spice jar)
- pieces of broken glass
- steel wool
- 3 strips of red cloth or ribbon
- a tack

1. Place all the ingredients into the jar and seal the lid.
2. Traditionally a bottle like this would be placed on the victim's property. If this is impossible, you can shake the bottle for 5 minutes a day while reciting the victim's name repeatedly.

4. Cause Insanity

- a piece of the victim's hair
- tinfoil

1. Wrap the hair in the tinfoil, pushing the foil away from yourself.
2. Throw the package into a running river or stream. It must be *running water* for this trick to have any effect.

5. Jinxing By Candle

- victim's photograph
- cayenne pepper
- a black candle OR a white candle covered in black shoe polish

1. Place the photo on a plate, tray, or whatever altar space you wish to use.
2. Draw an X over the photo with the cayenne pepper.
3. Place the candle on top of the picture and the spice. Light it while saying aloud your wish.
4. Let the candle burn all the way out.

CHAPTER EIGHT
Money Spells

Money is a major concern in most people's lives. People who don't have it want it, people who do have it want more. Some folks will turn to money magic in order to achieve their financial dreams.

As with love spells, the magic shouldn't be treated like a magic lamp that you can just rub to have whatever you want instantly delivered. Money spells can do great things, but they will work in inconspicuous and natural ways using the path of least resistance. This usually means that you will discover ways to earn more money, or you might find a small increase in gambling wins or in friends willing to gift or lend you cash. It is unlikely that you will "get rich" off a lone money spell unless you were already close to achieving such a thing. If you must use magic as your way to riches, then you should be prepared to do many, many spells over a long period of time.

Thursday or Friday are the best days for money work. Wednesday and Saturday are also considered auspicious.

1. Bottle Spell for Money

- 1 bottle or jar with lid (such as a cleaned sauce bottle)
- 5 pennies
- 5 nickles
- 5 dimes
- 5 grains of dry rice OR kernels of dried corn
- 5 sesame seeds
- 5 cinnamon sticks
- 5 cloves
- 5 allspice berries
- 5 pecans OR almonds

1. Place all the ingredients into the bottle or jar. Cap it tightly.

2. Holding the bottle in your non-dominant hand, shake it back and forth continuously while reciting the following mantra: "Spices, money, seeds and grain/Make increase financial gain." Continue this for five minutes.

3. When done, take your bottle outside your house and bury it in the yard; or if you don't have a yard, use a potted plant with the bottle hidden in the dirt. Point the cap of the bottle towards your door so that the money can 'pour' in that direction.

2. Increase Gambling Luck

- chamomile (tea or dried herb)

1. Steep the chamomile in boiling water, and allow it to sit till the water is cold.
2. Strain the chamomile and reserve the water.
3. Use the water to wash your hands before going out to game.

3. Be Led To Money

- 21 coins of the same denomination (the higher the denomination, the better)
- a jar or other container

1. Begin this on the new moon.
2. Put the coins into the jar, and fill the jar with water. Close the jar tightly.
3. Leave the coins and water sitting until the full moon.
4. After the full moon, take the water and rub or spray it onto your shoes, so that they will lead you to money.

4. A Money Gris-Gris

- a square of green or yellow cloth, approx. 6" wide
- thyme
- cinnamon
- a $2 bill OR a St. Raymond holy card
- string or thread

1. Fold the bill or card up small, always folding the paper toward yourself to draw the influence your way.
2. Put the money or card, plus 1 teaspoon of each herb, into the center of the cloth.
3. Draw up the corners of the cloth together to make a sort of pouch. Use the string to tightly bind the pouch about one to two inches up from the base. Tie the string off with three knots.
4. Carry this gris-gris in your pocket or purse at all times to draw money.

5. Make Your Money Grow

- your favorite alcohol or perfume
- ground nutmeg
- paper money
- green ink pen

Take whatever paper money you have and prepare each note in the following way:

1. Sign your name on it with green ink under the name of the Secretary of the Treasury. In the four corners of the bill, write: $$¢¢$$

2. After you've written everything out, take a dash of powdered nutmeg and rub it over both sides of the bill. Shake off any excess – the bill should not look gritty or dusty.

3. Dot the four corners of each bill with the alcohol or perfume. Do not worry if this blurs or smears the ink.

4. Place the money in the palm of your left hand. Open your left hand palm up with the fingers pointing away from your body, then place your right hand across it, palm down with fingers pointing to your left. The money should be sandwiched between your two hands which are now arranged in an X shape.

5. While holding the money in this way, recite all of Psalm 23.

6. After the dressing ritual is complete, take this money and spend it. It will "signal" for other money to come your way.

Note. Some who practice such rituals insist that the money should only be spent in ways that are likely to increase your income, such as for business expenses. Others feel it is acceptable to spend the money in any normal way that you would usually spend it. What is agreed upon is that the money should *not* be spent just for the sake of spending it, such as in buying something that you'd never buy otherwise. Using pure logic it can be deduced that spending money needlessly will not enhance your financial situation.

6. Attract Money

- Earl Grey tea bags

1. Place a tea bag in your wallet or purse to attract money. Earl Grey tea is flavored with bergamot, which is said to be a money-draw.

NOTE: for best results, avoid any "fancy" blends of Earl Grey such as *Earl Grey with Lavender* or *Vanilla Earl Grey*, as these additional herbs can change the meaning of the bergamot.

7. A Money Drawing Floorwash

- 3 tablespoons gumbo file (spice)
- 3 cinnamon sticks
- half ounce lemongrass essential oil
- 3 tablespoons sugar
- 8 ounce jar of honey
- 10 ounce bottle Bay Rum cologne or aftershave
- an empty quart bottle

1. Put all of the lemongrass oil, the file, the cinnamon, sugar, Bay Rum and honey together into the quart jar. Shake well to combine.
2. Add two to four tablespoons of this mix to the scrub water when washing your floor. Use this wash regularly for best results.

8. A Lucky Nutmeg

- 1 whole nutmeg
- tin foil
- a slim knife or a drill
- a candle (green is best, white is next best.)

1. Take the nutmeg and bore a hole through the center, making a cavity. Don't allow your blade to pass through the other side.
2. Take a small amount of tinfoil, and roll it up. Cram it down into the hole you've made in the nutmeg.
3. Using the lit candle, drip some wax onto the nutmeg in order to seal shut the hole you've made.
4. Carry this nutmeg with you for enhanced luck in money affairs.

9. A Lucky Onion Hand

- 1 small red onion (note: this onion *must* be acquired through some method where you do not pay for it. Otherwise it won't be lucky.)
- ground cayenne pepper
- ground asafoetida (spice) OR epsom salt
- a leather chamois (car wash supplies)
- a pint bottle of whiskey
- string, thread or yarn.
- a knife

1. Bore a hole into the onion, making a cavity inside it.
2. Fill the hole with the cayenne and asafoetida powders.
3. Take the chamois and place the onion in its center. Wrap it tightly around the onion.
4. Secure the chamois by tightly wrapping the string just above the onion, making a stem or bag from the chamois.
5. Douse the bag in whiskey while stating aloud your intentions, e.g. "Bring me lots of money luck and success."

6. When you go to gamble, or do business, or any other money-related venture, carry this bag with you and rub your hands on it before starting.

10. Draw Money To Business

- Florida Water cologne
- a green towel or rag
- a spray bottle

1. At your place of business, dampen your towel with Florida Water and begin to recite Psalm 1.
2. While reciting, wipe around the cash register (or whatever you use to hold the money.)
3. Continue to wipe anything else that customers will use – chairs, doors, shelves, counters, etc.
4. Put some of the cologne in the spray bottle and, three times weekly, spray some more of the cologne around your shop.

Note. Florida Water is an inexpensive cologne. It might be located with the Hispanic goods at your local store. If no shops near you carry Florida Water, you can instead use another perfume that you consider to be lucky. There will often be images on packages of cologne to help you see which ones are auspicious – look for pictures of horseshoes, dollar signs or money, diamonds, gold, etc.

CHAPTER NINE
Success Spells

Financial success is effectively another form of money spell, but there are some situations where one needs a sense of success for reasons that are not purely monetary. For instance, you may need to be accepted into a school, or build a reputation in a career, or just have a "successful party" where everyone enjoyed themselves.

A success spell is not a replacement for actually doing work, nor can you simply cast a success spell on a worthless cause and expect to transform it into a winner. A sow's ear is not a silk purse, nor can it ever be. A success spell simply makes the world around you more attuned and receptive to your project's benefits.

The best day to perform a success spell is on Sunday.

1. A Success Gris-Gris

- a square of white paper, about 5"x 5" or smaller
- a gold ink pen
- a small carrying case (no larger than the gris-gris, whatever style you like.)

1. On Sunday during the planetary hour of the Sun, write out the following rows of numbers on your paper:

   06 32 03 34 35 01
   07 11 27 28 08 30
   19 14 16 15 23 24
   18 20 22 21 17 13
   25 29 10 09 26 12
   36 05 33 04 02 31

2. Flip the paper and on the back draw a picture of a king seated in a throne, with a lion resting at his feet.

3. Put the paper into the carrying case. You may, if desired, fold or roll the paper to make it fit.

4. Carry this gris-gris charm with you, especially if you are undertaking any actions related to the project you want success for.

2. A Homemade Success Candle

- 2 white candles (freestanding)
- ½ teaspoon each ground allspice, ground orange peel, ground cinnamon
- a red crayon (or blue, orange, purple or yellow)

In a double-boiler, melt one candle and the crayon together till liquid.

To the liquid, add the spices and stir well. Remove mixture from heat.

Coat the second candle with the liquid wax mixture. This can be done by *quickly* dipping the candle into the wax liquid, or by pouring the liquid over the candle.

Allow the candle to cool. The finished candle can be burnt over a petition paper for your intent, or lit as you speak your desires aloud.

3. A Simple Bath for Success

- dried basil

1. Purchase a bottle of dried basil in the spice aisle. These bottles usually amount between 0.5 ounces and 0.75 ounces of herb.
2. Boil the whole bottle's contents in a pan of bubbling hot water for nine minutes.
3. After nine minutes, strain the liquid.
4. Add the resulting basil-water to your bath. Bathe in this mixture, scrubbing your body upwards with the water.
5. When you are done with the bath, reserve a cupful of the used bathwater.
6. At the next sunrise, go outdoors and toss the cup of bathwater towards the sunrise and say, "As the sun rises in the east, so shall my work give rise to success."

4. A Petition For Success

- a launching toy (toy stores carry many varieties of these gun-like items, designed to shoot small objects ranging from marshmallows to potatoes. Choose whatever make seems appropriate and will launch an object the size of a wadded sheet of paper.)
- a paper
- a pen

1. Take the paper and write out your wishes and requests for success with an ink pen.
2. Wad up the paper and load it into your launching toy.
3. Get up just before sunrise, and as the sun comes up over the horizon, fire the petition paper directly into the rising sun.

5. Walk Into Success

- 2 bay leaves

1. Take the bay leaves and lay one into each of your shoes. Put on the shoes, and wear the around with confidence that you'll be led into success.

CHAPTER TEN
Uncrossing Spells

"Uncrossing" is the term used by many hoodoo practitioners when referring to curse removal. In old-fashioned hoodoo thought, virtually any incident of bad luck was considered to be caused by a curse because a person's natural condition was felt to be lucky. Newer hoodoo thinking acknowledges that some misfortune is natural in life, and dismisses the idea that folks are casting malignant spells on one another at all times – but it still places a high regard on uncrossing spells, with some people feeling that they're still needed on a regular basis to prevent an accumulation of "negative energy" from various sources.

The best days for uncrossing spells are Sunday, Monday, Wednesday and, if you are trying to punish the one who put the spell on you to start with, Tuesday.

1. Unhexing Wash

- salt
- ground pepper
- ammonia

1. Add a tablespoon of each ingredient to your bath water.
2. Get in the bath and wash only in a downward motion. Be sure to wet your head with the bath water.

2. To Cure a Person Sickened By Conjure

- 1 cup water reserved from a bath of the afflicted
- hair of the afflicted
- fingernail clippings of the afflicted
- unwashed clothing of the afflicted
- 1 cup cornmeal (any color)
- a mortar and pestle
- a frying pan
- fat for frying

While this working would probably help with any kind of bad luck caused by a jinx, it is particularly commended for cases of "unnatural illness." These are sicknesses that are caused by malefic magic, and can usually be identified due to their inability to be treated with traditional medicine.

1. Perform this spell on the dark of the moon.
2. In a mortar and pestle, grind to a powder the hair and nail clippings.
3. Stir the dust and the cornmeal together.
4. If the bath water is not still warm, heat it back up. Add this to the cornmeal. The resulting mixture should be able to form a stiff dough.

5. Heat the pan with enough fat in it to cover the bottom ⅛ inch.

6. Shape the dough into a little loaf, and when the fat is sizzling, fry each side of the loaf till crusty and brown.

7. Take the bread from the heat and wrap it up in some unwashed clothing belonging to the victim.

8. Take the bread to a flowing river and, at the stroke of midnight, toss the bundle into the water.

Note. If it is impossible for you to find a body of moving water (a common problem for those who live in desert areas) then it is acceptable to toss the bundle into a crossroads.

3. To Deal With Found Conjure

- a cloth bag (drawstring is best, or you can use a rubberband or string to close the sack.)
- yeast powder
- a rare-earth magnet

If you believe you have found an item that was used to create a hex on you, take the item and do the following:

1. Place it into a cloth bag along with a tablespoon of yeast and a magnet.
2. Close the bag.
3. Take it to a river and cast it into the running water.

Note. A crossroads may be used if a river is not available.

4. Another Uncrossing Bath

- a box of salt
- a bundle of fresh herbs (these can be had from produce departments: mint, basil, parsley, cress are all common to find.)

1. Draw a bath and pour the entire box of salt into the bath water.
2. Take the bath, wash yourself.
3. Stand up in the tub and use the bundle of herbs to "whip" yourself, going in a downward motion over your body from the neck down.
4. When done, drain the tub and dispose of the remaining herbs by tossing them in your backyard or behind your house.

Note. If the crossed condition is very strong or stubborn, repeat this bath daily for nine days.

5. A Dry Bath To Uncross

- 1 ounce crushed camphor OR 13 drops camphor essential oil
- 1 quart cornmeal
- 2 lbs salt
- an old newspaper or other liner
- photo of the one who cast the curse (if known)

1. Combine the camphor, cornmeal and salt together in a bowl.
2. Spread out the newspaper to cover an area of the floor. If you have a photograph of the person who did the spell, lay that on the paper as well.
3. Stand on the newspaper and, if applicable, on the photo of the witch.
4. Taking handfuls of the cornmeal mix, rub your body from the scalp downwards to the feet with the powder. Let the mixture fall down to the newspaper.
5. After having used all of the mixture to dry-bathe, gather up the newspaper with all the powder still on it.
6. Take the newspaper, photo and powder, at midnight, to a crossroads. Leave it there, and don't look back.

6. An Uncrossing Floor Sweep

- 1 - 5 cups dried basil, depending on size of the house (large amounts like this can be bought in bulk herbs or from restaurant suppliers)
- basil essential oil

1. Scatter the basil over the floors of your house or any other place where you suspect a curse has been laid or is being affected by evil.
2. Allow the basil to sit for at least 30 minutes. While you wait, you can go around and put one or two drops on all the *cold, unlit* lightbulbs in your home.
3. Return and sweep or vacuum all the floors to collect the basil.
4. Afterwards, turn on all the lights and let the scent of the basil oil continue to purify the home.

Note. An identical floor sweep can be done with salt instead of basil.

7. A Cleansing Ritual

- 1 chicken egg
- nettle or peppermint tea
- incense (use a refreshing scent like rosemary or eucalyptus, or an all-purpose scent like Nag Champa.)
- laundry bluing or blue food coloring

1. Begin by brewing up a cup of nettle or peppermint tea. Drink the tea by itself in preparation for your ritual – do not add sweeteners or accompany it with snacks.
2. Set up in a private space like a bathroom or bedroom. Light your incense and have your egg ready.
3. Undress at least down to your underwear. Take the egg in your hand and begin rubbing it, in long sweeping strokes, across your body. Try to sweep the egg over every part of your body. Work downward from the head to the feet.
4. Optionally, as you perform this, you can recite 1 Timothy 1:17 – "Now to the King eternal, immortal, invisible, to God who alone is wise, be honor and glory forever, Amen." If you don't want to say this for whatever reason, you may instead declare aloud your wishes to be uncrossed.

5. Repeat the egg sweep from head to toe at least three times. If you egg breaks before completion, start over with a new egg.

6. When done, dispose of the egg by throwing it in the toilet (hard enough to break) and shutting the lid without looking at it, then flushing it away. Alternately, you can take the egg outdoors and throw it against a good, strong tree to absorb the bad energy.

7. To finish the ritual, draw a warm bath and add a teaspoon of laundry blueing or blue food color to the tub. Soak and wash in this blue liquid for 30 minutes, then drain the tub.

8. Kill Conjure That's Directed At You

- ground cayenne pepper
- salt
- Tiger Balm OR VapoRub

1. Combine the salt and cayenne. Sprinkle this in the four corners of your bedroom while speaking aloud your command that it remove any conjure or evil spells.
2. Open the pot of Tiger Balm or VapoRub, and place it under the bed. Leave it there and do not disturb it.
3. Leave both the powders and the ointment in place for at least 7 days – longer if you feel you need it. If you will keep it longer than 30 days, refresh the powders and ointment at least once per month.

9. A Simple Spell-Remover

- 1 bag of St. John's Wort tea
- 1 bag of Verveine or Verbena tea

1. Carry the two bags of tea together in your pocket at all times, to do away with any magic aimed your way. If you don't have pockets, you can string the bags on a necklace and wear it under your clothing.
2. Repeat this daily, with fresh tea bags, till a perfect cure is obtained.

10. To Remove A Curse And Punish the Witch

- your own urine (see instructions)
- your toenail clippings
- 3 of your hairs
- 9 garlic cloves
- 9 nails
- 10 pins
- a heart cut out of construction paper
- a quart pan with a lid (you will have to dispose of this as part of the spell – buy a cheap pan just for the purpose.)

1. Collect your first urine of the day for 3 days in a large jar or bottle.
2. In your pan, put the collected urine, the hair, nails, and bring to a boil.
3. While waiting for the mixture to boil, take the paper heart. This represents the heart of whatever person put the spell on you. If you know who the culprit was, write their name on it with ink. Pierce this paper heart with one of your pins, to represent a counter-attack.

4. When the urine is boiling, add to it the garlic, pins, nails and the paper heart. Let everything cook together over the heat until it boils dry.

5. When done, turn off the heat. Remove the pan from the stove, and put the lid over it. Seal down the lid with tape.

6. Take the pan outside your house and bury it; or if you do not have a yard, hide it somewhere in the house where it won't be seen or disturbed. This serves as a cure for the crossed condition, protection against future attacks, and revenge against the witch who did the spell on you.

CHAPTER ELEVEN
Protection Spells

Spells for protection are often used to guard against being jinxed or enchanted by magic. Some protective spells can also be used to avoid more mundane problems, like trouble with the police or unwelcome visitors.

As with all spells, protective magic should not be considered a replacement for common sense and should not be used instead of medicine, legal assistance, good behavior, etc. No magic spell can promise a 100% success rate, so don't think that a spell to protect against disease will make it a good idea to toss out all your prescription medicines, or that a spell to protect against harm is a replacement for being cautious and seeking help from the authorities when needed, etc. etc.

Protective work can best be done on Mondays, Tuesdays and Saturdays.

1. Protect Yourself From Witchcraft

- cayenne pepper
- salt

Combine the two powders and sprinkle a little of them in your shoes every day. You can also sprinkle this powder at the four corners of your house or your bed for more protection.

2. Protect The Home From Misfortune

- white or yellow mustard seed

Sprinkle the seed in front of the doors of your house to keep away enemies, evade witches, and kill harmful spells.

3. Hex-Proof Your Home

- cayenne pepper powder
- household ammonia
- laundry bluing OR blue food color
- a dish (a pretty, decorative one is recommended)
- 3 eggshells, dried and crushed into fine powder

1. Begin by mixing a bucket of floorwash with enough bluing to color the water, and 3 drops of ammonia. Wash the floors with this mixture, and if you have one, the front porch or walkway.

2. When the floors are clean and dry, take the red powder outside your front door and sprinkle it just outside the threshold. You may conceal the dust underneath a doormat if desired.

3. Take the dish and fill it with water, then add enough bluing to tint the water deep blue. Set this dish behind your front door, inside the house.

4. Take the powdered eggshell on your fingertips and draw a cross or an X on the door with it (don't worry if the shape is not strongly visible.) This completes the protection. Repeat this procedure at least every 2 weeks to maintain.

4. Guard Yourself Against Spells And Evil Eye

- a string of blue beads OR black beads (if you can't find a necklace or bracelet already strung, craft stores will carry such beads for making your own.)

Wear this string of beads on your body (it doesn't need to be visible to others) to guard against witchcraft or negative energies.

5. A Protective Gris-Gris

- a strip of paper
- a black ink pen
- a wallet, coin-purse or other carrier

1. With the pen, you should write out as carefully as possible the following onto the strip of paper:

الَّذِينَ قَالَ لَهُمُ النَّاسُ إِنَّ النَّاسَ قَدْ جَمَعُوا لَكُمْ

فَاخْشَوْهُمْ فَزَادَهُمْ إِيمَانًا وَقَالُوا حَسْبُنَا اللَّهُ

وَنِعْمَ الْوَكِيلُ

These words mean, "Men said to them: 'A great army is gathering against you': And frightened them: But it increased their Faith: They said: 'For us Allah sufficeth, and He is the best disposer of affairs.'" This is a traditional gris-gris of the oldest historical type, used for protection.

2. Take the paper and place it in your container. Keep it always with you.

6. Protection From Witchcraft While Sleeping

- an egg
- a permanent marker

1. Take the egg and write your name on it with the marker.

2. Locate a spot in your bedroom that is about the same level as your head will be when sleeping. Place the egg in this spot.

3. Sleep, and know you are protected – any witchcraft sent your way will go to the egg instead. If the egg breaks, throw it out and prepare a new egg. Change the egg weekly whether it breaks or not.

7. Protection Against Police Visits

- sterling silver charms (these can be had from craft stores – any shape will do, the silver is what's important.)
- small nails
- hammer
- blue sand (available in craft stores or in toy stores) OR sand gathered from a beach at the point where the water meets the land.

Note. You need as many silver charms as you have windows in your house, and a nail for securing each.

- Above every window of the house, nail one of your silver charms.
- Take a handful of the blue sand and scatter it inside the front doorway. Repeat for any other doors that lead outside. Refresh the sand weekly, for as long as needed.

8. Against Unwanted Suitors

- black cohosh root OR fennel seed (bulk herbs, teas, or spices)
- citronella essential oil

1. Allow the herb to steep in boiling water for at least 30 minutes.
2. Strain the herb and reserve the liquid infusion.
3. Add the infusion to your bath water. Bathe for at least 30 minutes.
4. After the bath, use a drop of citronella as your perfume.
5. Wear the citronella perfume daily and repeat the bath weekly, for as long as necessary.

9. Protection From Disease

- 9 bundles of fresh or dried chives, secured with rubberbands or twine.

1. The herb bundles can either be let to rest on the floor concealed by some object, or can be strung up from the ceiling or hung on the wall. Place a bundle of chives in the four corners inside your home (if your home is not perfectly square or is oddly shaped, just choose the four most distant areas of the house.)

2. Place the remaining bundles in areas of the house you feel are vulnerable, such as bedrooms or near doors.

3. Refresh the herb bundles every 3 months for continued effect.

10. Protection From A Bully

- image of St. Michael (a holy card, medal, or a printed image from your computer will do)
- 10 white candles, unscented
- olive oil
- 10 sticks or cones of incense – a traditional scent like frankincense, rose or sandalwood is recommended
- salt (kosher salt is best)
- black cloth
- string or twine
- a personal item of the bully's OR a photo of the bully

1. Set up an altar space, ideally where you can leave everything undisturbed for the full ten days this ritual will take. Put out the image of Michael, and set the black cloth in front of it. Put the bully's item on the cloth.

2. Dress a candle with olive oil and set it beside the image of Michael. Put the incense next to the image as well.

3. Light the candle and incense and aloud ask Michael for his help in ending the bully's reign of terror.

4. Use the salt to draw an X over the bully's item. Allow the candle and incense to burn out.

5. Each day, burn another olive-dressed candle and piece of incense for Michael, repeating your petition each time.

6. After the final day, wrap up the item and the salt together inside the black cloth. Secure the wrapping with the twine or string.

7. Take the bundle to a deep lake, stream or other body of water, and drop the packet into it to represent that the bully is 'sunk'; or, if there's no water near you, you can put the bundle into a plastic container and fill it ¾ with water, making sure the bundle is submerged. Hide the container in the back of your freezer and never disturb it – this 'freezes' the bully and makes sure he can no longer act to harm you.

11. Protect Against Gossip

- clove essential oil OR mint essential oil OR fennel essential oil

1. Use the oil as a home fragrance to ward away malicious gossip concerning you. You can burn it in special oil diffusers, or apply a drop to any *cold, unlit* lightbulbs in the house and then turn them on so the increasing heat of the bulb warms the oil and spreads the scent.

2. You can also use the oil as a personal perfume, to discourage gossip about yourself when you're away from the house, by mixing a few drops into your usual perfume or body lotion and combining well before use.

CHAPTER TWELVE
Luck Spells

Good luck might be the most important thing to have of all the thing there are – when we have plenty of good luck, we suffer from fewer problems in general and don't need to focus on love or money or protection since it will come to us naturally and without effort. Our lives will flow smoothly, we will make friends instead of enemies, be healthy and happy, and be successful in our ventures.

Wednesday and Thursday are especially lucky days for performing this type of spell, according to the planetary system of magic.

1. To Bring Luck To A House

- old, used shoes (you can use a worn out pair of your own, or find a discarded pair)
- sugar
- salt

You will need a working fireplace with chimney to perform this spell.

1. Just before dawn, start to build up a fire and get a hot flame going.
2. When the fire is roaring, and as the sun is rising, toss the shoes onto the fire, then a handful each of salt and sugar on top. As you toss in each item, say aloud "Shoes/salt/sugar, bring me the best of luck!"
3. Be certain to let the shoes burn into ashes.

2. Have Good Luck

- 3 star anise pods

Carry the pods in your pocket or purse every day for good luck.

3. Attract Good Fortune To Your Home

- ground cinnamon
- salt
- ground allspice

1. Combine these three powders.
2. Sprinkle the mixture in all the entrances of your house. As you do, say, "Come in, come in, come in!" This attracts in Luck.

4. "Chinese Wash" For Luck

- 9 drops tincture of benzoin (health/medical supplies)
- 9 drops citronella essential oil
- 3 tsp unscented liquid castile soap
- 9 cups hot water
- a new broom (one made from natural straws is best)

1. Combine all ingredients in a bucket.
2. Use the resulting mixture as a floor wash for the house, but instead of a mop, use the broom to scrub the floors with the liquid. If there is a porch or walkway, wash them as well. If at all possible, you should wash the house going inward (from front to back), to represent the luck being pulled into the house.
3. After washing the home, take the dirty water that remains in the bucket to the nearest crossroads and pour it out there. Return home without looking back.

NOTE: If your home has wall to wall carpeting, you can still perform a version of this spell, though it will not be as strong. Mix the liquid ingredients and a fresh few broom straws, put them into a spray bottle, and spritz them around the home like an air freshener spray, working front to back.

5. A Lucky Jackball

- your hair
- tinfoil
- sand from the point where the water meets the shore OR blue sand (available in crafts or kids departments)
- 3 lengths (48" each) of white embroidery floss
- 3 lengths (48" each) of white yarn
- a square of white cloth, paper or a napkin
- a package of chewing tobacco
- a pint of whiskey
- a yarn needle

This is adapted from a very old ritual. Jackballs are a style of magic charm made from wound yarn or string, believed to contain the *soul* of the person they were made for. Caring for a jack is serious business – do not make this talisman lightly!

1. Three days before starting, combine the chewing tobacco and whiskey in a separate bottle and let them soak together. Have this liquid at ready when you begin making the jack.
2. Take each length of the thread and tie 4 knots into it, while speaking aloud, "For [your name], that s/he have friends and allies." Dip the thread into the whiskey each time.
3. Repeat the process for the lengths of yarn as for the

thread, so again each length will have 4 knots, "For [your name], that s/he be protected from evil." Dip the yard into the whiskey each time.

4. Start reciting your prayer aloud (e.g. "I conjure you spirits to bring me luck.") Take your square of cloth or paper, and place the bit of your hair, a small piece of foil, and a teaspoon of the sand upon it. Wrap it up together into a tight wad.

5. Moisten the paper or cloth with the whiskey mixture.

6. Take a length of yarn and thread together. Start wrapping the yarn around the bundle, repeating your prayer all the while. It is recommended one begin with an X shape, and then continue wrapping round and round, repeating your prayer.

7. Repeat with a new length of yarn and thread together, wrapping and praying, and do this till all the lengths of yarn and thread are used and the ball is entirely covered so the contents are no longer visible. Leave a long length of the yarn loose.

8. Using a yarn needle, thread the remaining yarn, and stitch it back through the ball to create a hanging loop.

9. Tie off this loop at the base with three knots, repeating the prayer at the tying of each knot. Remove the needle and snip off any excess thread still hanging.

10. Baptize your ball in the whiskey one more time and declare aloud that the jack is complete, and remind it of its purpose to bring luck, happiness, fortune, friendship, etc.

11. Carry the jack with you always. Jacks are considered to be alive and should be fed regularly; once a week you should moisten it with more of the tobacco-

whiskey mix. If you need spiritual guidance or need extra boosts of luck, hold the jack by its string and ask it your question; it will make some sign of its reply.

Note. If you cannot acquire whiskey or tobacco, it is acceptable to use a lucky perfume instead (see Money Spell #10 for more information.)

CHAPTER THIRTEEN
Miscellaneous Spells

1. Four Thieves Vinegar, for Harm or Protection

This mixture was originally created as an antiseptic, tonic and perfume, used to guard against disease. Folklore gives many fanciful accounts of its creation, but a mixture by this name appears to have originated no earlier than the 18th century. By the early 20th century, hoodoo practitioners were using it in harmful magic to soak candles, papers and other items that would be used in the spellcast.

You can use Four Thieves Vinegar either as a protective mixture or as a harmful one. Here is a simple, modern style recipe:

- a pint of vinegar (any type, though wine vinegars are most traditional)
- Any four of the following: edible camphor, cinnamon, mint, juniper berries, lavender, rosemary, sage, clove, garlic, nutmeg

Combine a tablespoon of each herb with the vinegar, and let these sit together for one month. Strain out the herbs and use the resulting vinegar mix. Some manufacturers like to add food coloring to enhance the power – see Chapter Four for instructions about colors.

2. Hungary Water, for Health, Beauty and Purification

This early form of cologne was originally made from distilled rosemary flowers. It was used as a muscle balm, a tonic, a toner, an antiseptic, a mouthwash and of course as a plain old perfume – in effect, it was considered a cure-all. A simple version can be made at home.

- 2 ounces Everclear or 91% isopropyl alcohol
- 15 drops rosemary essential oil
- 10 drops lavender essential oil
- 5 drops petitgrain essential oil (optional)

Combine all and mix well. Keep bottled tightly.

3. To Have Prophetic Visions

- a poppyseed bagel
- a hat or box or dark cloth

This bagel will serve as a seer stone – you can see the future in the center hole.

- Take the bagel and put it into a hat or box or dark cloth to obscure surrounding light. The bagel should be very much in the dark, so that you can barely see it. Focus intently on the bagel while bearing in mind what you wish to see information about. If you have the talent, you will be able to see some indication of whatever you wish, though you may need to practice this technique several times before getting results.

4. To Make Hair Grow Long

Trim the ends of your hair during the full moon or waxing moon. Collect all the hair trimmings and bury them outside in a damp, sunny spot such as where plants would thrive and flourish. This has been said to cause your hair to grow in a similar manner to the plants.

5. To Be Popular and Loved

- lavender essential oil
- salt
- Gold Bond powder (the kind in the yellow bottle is preferred)
- patchouli oil or perfume

1. Take a bath adding 10 drops lavender oil and a heaping handful of salt to the bath water. Stay in the bath for 30 minutes.
2. After the bath, it is ideal to let yourself air dry, though you can wrap yourself in a towel or robe to prevent drips.
3. When dry, lightly dust your body with the Gold Bond powder.
4. Scent your pulse points with the patchouli oil or perfume.

For best results, this should be repeated thrice weekly for as long as needed. Monday, Wednesday and Friday are the best days to do it.

Note. This can be enhanced if used alongside the Chinese Wash Luck spell given in the previous chapter.

6. To Visit Someone In Dreams

- white candle
- a knife or a pin
- Nag Champa OR Sandalwood OR Anise incense
- a mirror

Naturally, the best time to do this is at an hour when you believe your target will be sleeping. Perform this is a room with no other artificial light but the candle.

1. Carve the name of your target onto the candle backwards (mirrored) with the knife or pin.
2. Face the direction you believe your target to be in, and set the white candle and incense in front of you, and the mirror behind them. Light the candle and incense.
3. Get into a comfortable position which you'll be satisfied to remain fixed in for a length of time.
4. Begin by noticing your image in the mirror. Close your eyes if required, and spend as much time as needed transferring your consciousness from your body into your mirror image. When you can clearly see yourself (natural body) sitting before you on the opposite side of the candle and incense, and the name on the candle reads in the correct (unmirrored)

122

direction, you'll have succeeded. Note that this may take some time – even experienced practitioners might need as much as 15 minutes.

5. You are now astrally traveling in mirror world. Your target probably has a mirror somewhere in their home, maybe even in their bedroom. Find it, and bring yourself to exit through that nearby mirror, and proceed to their bed where they sleep.

6. Exit the mirror and go to your target's bedside. Stand over them and do to them whatever you need to do: talk to them or perform actions on them. Remind them that they're dreaming, in order to keep them asleep.

7. Return the way you came – through the mirror, back to the mirror which you placed in front of your natural body, where you can see yourself.

8. Use every effort to bring your consciousness properly and securely back to your natural body before you conclude the ritual.

9. When you are done and are stable in your body, blow out the candle (if any remains) and discard it. Do not use it again for any other purpose.

Note. If your target has magical protection, such as those in Chapter 11, you might be unable to succeed at this.

A NOTE TO THE USER

Though efforts have been made to only list commonly available ingredients for the spells in this book, it will doubtless occur that some people will still be unable to acquire some ingredients for whatever reason. If it happens to you, and you cannot find the ingredient you need for the spell you want, and no logical replacement presents itself to you, then it is a sign that you should try a different spell.

Made in the USA
Columbia, SC
17 October 2020

22975391R00070